The Cradle of
THE ARYANS

MAVEN BOOKS

The Cradle of
THE ARYANS

Gerald H. Rendall

MAVEN BOOKS

Chennai　　　Trichy　　　Tirunelveli　　　New Delhi

An Imprint of **MJP Publishers**

ISBN 978-93-90063-21-5 **Maven Books**

All rights reserved   No. 44, Nallathambi Street,
Printed and bound in India   Triplicane, Chennai 600 005

MJP 872   © Publishers, 2020

Publisher : C. Janarthanan

Publisher's Note

The legacy of a country is in its varied cultural heritage, historical literature, developments in the field of economy and science. The top nations in the world are competing in the field of science, economy and literature. This vast legacy has to be conserved and documented so that it can be bestowed to the future generation. The knowledge of this legacy is slowly getting perished in the present generation due to lack of documentation.

Keeping this in mind, the concern with retrospective acquiring of rare books has been accented recently by the burgeoning reprint industry. Maven Books is gratified to retrieve the rare collections with a view to bring back those books that were landmarks in their time.

In this effort, a series of rare books would be republished under the banner, "Maven Books". The books in the reprint series have been carefully selected for their contemporary usefulness as well as their historical importance within the intellectual. We reconstruct the book with slight enhancements made for better presentation, without affecting the contents of the original edition.

Most of the works selected for republishing covers a huge range of subjects, from history to anthropology. We believe this reprint edition will be a service to the numerous researchers and practitioners active in this fascinating field. We allow readers to experience the wonder of peering into a scholarly work of the highest order and seminal significance.

Maven Books

PREFACE.

THE following Essay is a paper originally communicated, necessarily in abridged form, to the members of the Liverpool *Literary and Philosophical Society*, and is an attempt to give a clear account of present controversies regarding the origin, local and racial, of the Aryan stock. It makes no claim to original discoveries in the field of language; but it embodies the results of somewhat extensive reading, mainly in German authorities; it gives a much fuller account than as yet exists in English of the latest Continental theories; and it presses some conclusions and inferences to what appears to me their legitimate issue, more closely than has been done by previous writers. I give it separate publication, thinking it may be of use to other students in the field of language. The better to fulfil this end, in the sections dealing with vocabulary I have systematically inserted in brackets some familiar representative of the term discussed; where this is not done, it is to be understood that the English word itself represents the stem in question. This, with the comparative tables introduced, will make it easy to check etymological statements, without uncertainty and loss of time. To gain compactness, I have refrained from not a few tempting digressions, and confined myself to categorical statement, with or without supporting reference in the notes. I have not needlessly multiplied citations, but every one acquainted with the literature of the subject will perceive my obligations to Max Müller, especially in his *Biographies of Words* and *The Home of the Aryas;* to Penka, *Origines Ariacæ* and *Herkunft der Arier;* to Schrader *Sprachvergleichung und Urgeschichte;* and in somewhat less degree to Spiegel *Die Arische Periode.* I hope no material point advanced by Benfey, Geiger, Hehn, Lenormant, Van den Gheyn, or among English writers by Latham, Sayce, Whitney and others, has escaped me. Much of Pictet is by general consent obsolete. For comparative etymology I have leaned, as must every student, on Fick's *Vergleichendes Wörterbuch der Indo-Germanischen Sprachen,* using the 3rd ed. (1876), and checking results by the useful lists in Max Müller's *Biographies of Words,* and by the stricter canons of modern etymology.

TABLE OF CONTENTS.

THE CRADLE OF THE ARYANS.

I. *The Indo-Europeans and their Habitat.*

WHEN, in the closing years of the last century, Sir W. Jones discovered to the Western world the secret of Sanskrit and taught them that in the far East, the accepted cradle of the human race, there existed a language of immemorial antiquity, the germs of which showed unmistakable identity with European speech at large, it seemed for a moment as though the primitive, perhaps the universal, language of mankind had been unearthed, and India was its home. Study, analysis, and reflection soon dispelled the dream; and the true character of the great Indo-European unity, which Schlegel was perhaps the first to apprehend, was established by the genius and industry of Bopp, who mapped out for all time the broad general demarcations which define the separate groups of closely correlated families of speech. Students of language have ever since that time been busily engaged in cross-questioning the evidence of language, and trying to extort thence the secret of the prehistoric movements, culture, and dwelling-places of Indo-European man.

The first crude hypothesis of an Indian origin was soon found untenable. It was exchanged for the theory, propounded by Pott, and brilliantly elaborated by Pictet, that the true home of the stock was to be found in the Bactrian plains of Central Asia; and this general theory, in forms variously modified, may be said to have held the field without serious dispute until quite recent years. The theory had much to commend it. It gave a compact and simple scheme to philologists, already wedded on the strength of historical and biblical * prepossessions to the assumption of an Eastern descent; it brought the Eranian and Indian stocks, whose languages seemed to stand closest to the parent speech, locally nearest to the cradle of the race; it assumed the continuous migration westward, which, while admitting simple and intelligible diagrammatical presentment, tallied agreeably with accredited beliefs; it could be brought without much violence to explain the seeming ratio of divergence shown by the derivative languages from the parent stock; and it conveniently located the primitive Aryan in districts inaccessible and unknown. It is still maintained in general outline by such veteran authorities as Fick, Hehn, Kiepert, and Max Müller, as well as by a crowd of lesser lights; but within the last ten years the new heresy that advocates a European origin has everywhere gained ground, and now threatens to chase its adversary from the field. The somewhat random guess first hazarded by Latham † in 1854, can no longer ‡ be set aside as the fancy of a hare-brained Englishman of "the land of curiosities," or the adopted whim of a Göttingen Professor. One may smile at eccentricities or extravagances of argument in Geiger or Cuno, or at Pösche's strange preference for the Rokitno swamps traversed by the Dnieper, the Beresina, and the Pripet; but it is impossible to set aside such names as Benfey, Spiegel, Schrader, or in our own language, Whitney, Sayce, and Taylor. Members of this Society may welcome a clear account of the controversy as it now stands.

---

* The Semitic tradition is valueless for the determination of Aryan descent, but how strong a hold it still has may be seen in Van den Gheyn, *L'Origine Europ. des Aryas*, p. 17–19.

† First, in his *Native Races of the Russian Empire*, 1854; more deliberately in *Elements of Comparative Philology* (1862).

‡ As in 1874 by Hehn, *Culturpflanzen u. Hausthiere*, referring to Latham and Benfey, and in a subsequent sentence to Geiger. The 1883 ed., 424 pp., treats the problem in a different tone.

II. *Indo-European Civilisation.*

Indecisive as for our purpose the results will be, it seems needful to rehearse the inferences gained from language regarding Indo-European culture prior to the separation of stocks. The material has been thrashed by many flails,[*] and brief recapitulation will suffice. Between the dashing constructiveness of Pictet, and the guarded scepticism of Hehn, there is a wide gulf; I shall content myself with results that seem secure. It will certainly be right to accept Max Müller's criterion that to vindicate its claim to Indo-European rights a word must find representation in at least one section of the Asiatic and one of the European groups, a distinction the validity of which Spiegel's *Die Arische Periode* has so irrefragably enforced. Over and above this the strictest canons demand—(1) that there should be correspondence between suffix as well as root, word-formation, that is to say, as well as derivation; otherwise mere prominence of some defining attribute may be misconstrued into a guarantee for its exemplification in some form really belonging to a later stage; *e.g.* **Sk.** *ragatá* beside ἄργ-υρος is a poor warrant for the Indo-European acquaintance with silver. (2) Even complete correspondences are sometimes insecure, and must never be pushed to implications belonging to a later period. **Sk.** *puri* by πόλις will prove only rude mound embankments, not the construction of walled cities, which are unknown to the Vedas; still less, to take verbal roots, does community in the root VAP prove weaving with the loom, or NA the invention of the needle. (3) Full allowance must be made for borrowed terms, and what is hardly less important, the borrowed application of existing terms. This caution applies specially

---

[*] For English statements see in particular Sayce, *Introduction to Science of Language ;* Lenormant, *Manual of Oriental History.*

in the consideration of implements, maritime, for instance, or agricultural. Such safeguards minimise necessarily the range allowed to Indo-European civilisation, and must be balanced by a frank recognition that deficient evidence can never *prove* ignorance or absence of the idea or thing desiderated. Because no common term has chanced to survive for river, or butter, or egg, or the human skin, no one would argue that any one of these was either unknown or unnamed.

Building on such canons of evidence, and omitting much that is unessential to the present enquiry, the following results seem secure. At the Indo-European stage of language, man had advanced beyond the savage predatory stage, which depends for existence on the bounties of nature and the spoils of river, plain, and forest. He was more than hunter and fisher. Animals were already distinguished into wild and tame. Already the sheep, the dog, *par excellence* the cow, and in all reasonable probability the horse, the pig, and the goat* had become the friends of man. To these the Eastern section, before their differentiation, added the mule, the ass, and possibly the camel, and the North European the reindeer. Of birds, the goose and duck were named, and perhaps domesticated, and the Easterns knew and possibly prized the hen. The general cast of the vocabulary implies (though negatively, it is true) an era of peace, and even at the much later stage, suggested by a comparison of Greek and Latin, there is a singular discrepancy between the terms that deal with war. The few common names for weapons may well represent nothing but man's primitive warfare with nature and wild beasts. The

---

* Hehn seems hypercritical in contesting the *domestication* of the horse and the goat, the more as archæology attests the fact at very early stages; but it matters little to the general controversy. Schrader excludes the pig and the horse from the ranks of the domesticated (*Sprachvergleichung*, &c., IV, cap. ii, with comparative table at pp. 350–1). Hehn satisfactorily traces the ass, mule, and fowl to the east. Spiegel supplies the common terms.

social instinct was developed, and men clustered in communities, owning forms of government, resting apparently on a patriarchal and monogamic * basis; family relationships, alike of blood and marriage, to the second and third degree, had attained a precision of definition that modern civilisation has virtually dispensed with. The mode of life was pastoral, the people tending herds and living on their produce. "Daughters" of the family, according to an approved etymology, † took their name from their daily work as milkers of the herd. How far boviculture was advanced, and how universal it was, is proved by the completeness of the vocabulary. Bull, ox, cow, heifer, calf, are all distinguished, and the equation Sk. *vádhri* = $\H{\epsilon}\theta\rho\iota\varsigma$ proves the systematic practice of castration. In two of the derived languages cattle supplied the measure of wealth. Flesh was eaten roast, marrow was gathered from the bones, and wild honey supplied a drink‡ that anticipated the more intoxicating efficacies of wine and beer. Agriculture was in its infancy; the culture of fruit trees is unattested, but one cereal at least was named, and in all probability cultivated.§ Ploughing

---

" So Benfey infers from $\pi\acute{o}\sigma\iota\varsigma$ and $\pi\acute{o}\tau\nu\iota\alpha$. Schrader, p. 198, demurs.

† The derivation from DUH, "suck," has rather better phonetic warrant (Schrader, p. 195), but Max Müller, in his B*iog. of Words*, still upholds the old etymology.

‡ Sk. *madhu.* Ale or beer is European, and the proof that wine is Indo-European is doubtful, resting on *vinum*, etc., compared with Arm. *gini*, Georg. *ghwino.* The word may be Semitic, see p. 35, as was the plant.

§ The one admitted equation is Sk. Zd. Slav. Lit. *jáva* = $\zeta\epsilon\iota\acute{a}$, &c. Both Hehn and Mommsen demur to the inference of systematic agriculture : but it is quite unlikely that the name of any wild product would have secured such widespread and persistent identity, and the weight of reason lies irresistibly with Benfey and Schrader, *Sprachv. u. Urgeschichte*, pp. 354-67, in vindicating a knowledge of agriculture for Indo-European man. The cumulative evidence of the words collected under Agriculture, in Max Müller's B*iographies of Words*, is decisive. As regards Zd. *gurt-ak* = $\kappa\rho\iota\theta\acute{\eta}$ = *hordeum*, and Sk. *sasá* = Zd. *hahya* = $\mathring{\eta}\iota\alpha$, it may with perfect right be urged that pastoral folk would have names for fodder, grass, and the like, prior to any deliberate agriculture.

and sowing were recognised operations; man, that is to say, had learned that seed should be scattered and sods turned; ruder implements at least, such as the waggon with roller wheels and axle, and the yoke, appropriate it will be observed to oxen as the animals for draught, the reaping-hook, and probably the mill-stone,* were at command. Further advances in agriculture are certified only for the European section, where much, that Mommsen † has worked out for Greeks and Italians in particular, is applicable to the group as a whole.

Building, weaving, planting, and navigation, however rudimentary their forms, were numbered among the arts: but 'building' may be limited to cave-dwellings, roofed burrows among the rocks, or rude huts of wood or wattle; 'weaving' to mere twisted network of osier, fibre or other raw material. For weapons, we are certified of the use of the spear, the axe, the sword, the bow and arrow, and in the East the club; but it is of special interest to know that more than one name explicitly records, and none refutes, its pre-metallic fabrication from wood, or bone, or stone. ‡ It is interesting to find the razor § (i.e., " scraper ") already in vogue. Copper (or, less probably, iron)‖ had attained distinction, but neither gold nor silver can be legitimately

---

* Sk. *malana* = *mola*, etc., the doubtful *kûrna* = γρῦ = *granum*, *dhăna* = Slav. *duna*, establish a presumption in favour of Indo-European grinding, but " quern " is specialised from a more general term for stone, and mill and its cognates from the generalised MAR = crush. As for reaping-hook, λᾶιον and O.N. *lẻ* by Sk. *lavi* seems decisive, though ἅρπη, Sl. *skupu* is European only.

† Mommsen, *Hist. Rome*, ch. ii.

‡ So in wood κῆλον and δόρυ by Sk. *dru*, in bone πέλεκυς by Sk. *parasú* (rib), and in stone ἄκων and ἄκμων (cf. German *hamar* and *sahs*).

§ *Kshurá*, ξυρόν, to which Benfey has devoted special essays. Denmark has yielded a razor from the early Bronze age. Montelius, *Civilisation of Sweden*, p. 60.

‖ On this see Max Müller, B*iographies &c.*, pp. 180–1, with App. V, 252 pp.

traced back to the Indo-European stage. * For science, if
the term is not too pretentious, numeration was definite up
to 100; sun, moon, and stars were observed, and the Great
Bear had received his name; broad divisions of the year
into seasons and months had gained recognition, though
language has nothing to suggest that the simple and obvious
lunar month had been adjusted to any maturer form of
annual calendar. The brighter colour contrasts were distinguished, speech had stepped into rhythm (an ingenious
inference of Westphal from the metrical use of 'foot'),† and
conscious appreciation of sounds foretold the charms of
melody. Religion, in the form of mythological beliefs, had
attained prolific growth.

The civilisation thus depicted may obviously have had its
home in Europe or in Asia. It stops far short of Pictet's
idyllic reconstructions ; it represents man emerging out of
neolithic savagery into the less intolerable disciplines of the
age of bronze.

Evidence so limited and fragmentary might not unna-
turally awaken some *prima facie* distrust of the results.
Interpretative imagination, it might be felt, the true his-
torian's gift, is needed to supplement methods too grudging
and too sceptical. But, on the whole, archæology and comparative anthropology remarkably confirm the order and proportion of development that the linguistic evidence suggests.
The range, for instance, of domestic animals, and even the
order of domestication, the priority of pastoral and nomadic
life to agricultural, the proportionate advance in building,
weaving, and the other arts, are all remarkably confirmed by
facts of archæology or savage life. A specific instance may

* To this vexed question Schrader has given exhaustive discussion,
Sprachvergleichung, Part III.
† Schrader, p. 199, protests, but the figure is too much out of the com-
mon for mere coincidence in Skt., Zd., and Gk.

be given in the fact that, while the primitive language distinguishes the more violent colours—red, yellow, white, and black—the finer grades (*sc.* of shorter wave-length), the recognition * of which indubitably comes later, find no Indo-European names. Throughout, there is coherence and proportion ; and if the evidence were far in arrear of the actual truth, some paradox of language would doubtless crop out, and inferentially reveal the unattested interspace.

III. *Climate, Fauna, and Flora.*

Of the results established by the earliest enquirers, none have proved more permanent than their conclusion regarding climatic environment. They disposed finally of the Indian supposition. The one defined season perpetuated in the vocabularies of all branches of Indo-European folk is *winter* (**Sk.** *himá*), and this, moreover, used in Eastern tongues to designate time, a winter season, not merely winter-cold. With it range the companion stems that designate snow and ice, shared by Eranian with European tongues. India has, indeed, lost names which lay outside her experience in things, but still exhibits the snow (*snih*) stem in the meaning ' shine.' For ' spring ' also (*ver*) there is a common term, but alike for ' summer ' and for ' autumn ' the stems that can claim to be Indo-European shew far more vagueness of definition, and in the Eastern group denote year or season in a general rather than specific sense. The fact that winter dominates the yearly reckoning, and firmly holds its place, even in torrid India, of necessity relegates the founders of Indo-European speech to some climate familiar with ice and snow, and winter's binding grip. To this condition Northern Europe and Central Asia conform with equal ease.

* The argument remains sound, if (as with some African tribes) recognition was extended only to the *colours found in cattle,* those of natural phenomena being unimportant and ignored.

Vocabulary next claims critical examination.

The term for 'sea' deserves preliminary handling. There is no common name. One word is European,* endorsed by Latin, Celtic, Slavonic, Lithuanian, and Teutonic stocks. The Eastern languages use different stems, and those distinct from one another, the Eranian *daraya* or *zaraya* only finding representation in India as denoting a flat plain. This may be mere accident; Greek has lost the word,† and turned to independent sources: and why not therefore Zend likewise and Sanskrit, just as no common term for 'river' is shared by East and West? Still the fact is striking. The sea is one of the phenomena likely to make a permanent impression on the mind, and win a name defying change or oblivion. And assuming some historic circumstance to underlie the divergence, what is the interpretation? The upholders of the Asiatic hypothesis set some store by the fact. The race, they say, was cradled in the interior. One branch, moving southwards, first found the sea on coasts of Persia and of India, and there devised new names for the new wonder; and so likewise the westward migration for itself, on gaining Europe and the sea. But the fact that *all* the European brotherhood (the Greeks excepted) share the same word, implies that the term was framed in common, not independently therefore on European shores, and the further inference is drawn that it was the Caspian Sea that supplied the new experience and the new name. The argument savours of perilous precision, and the unanimity of the European races in conservation of the term, as they pursued their distant inland routes, tempts to semi-credulous surprise. The alternative interpretation, say on Penka's reading, teaches that the word is an heirloom

* Mare, O.G. *more*, O.S. *morje*, Goth. *marei*, Lit. *mârė*, Ir. *muir*, Sl. *morje*. Fick and others find this in Sk. *mîra*, ocean, but Max Müller denies the identity.

† But possibly preserved in 'Αμφί-μαρος.

of the stock, first taught on Baltic shores ; that it survived in all the European tongues, but that, in the long pilgrimage and sojourn in the East, it was lost to the **Eranian vocabu-**lary, and a new term borrowed or devised by the Indians, and the first explorers of the Persian coast. In such a statement there is little forced or unnatural, though some small balance of plausibility rests with the former view. One solid inference remains, viz., that the language was not framed *in the interior of Europe*. The word must derive from some joint home upon some sea-board, whether of Europe, or peradventure of the Caspian or Aral seas.

The same may be said, though less forcibly, of the dis-crepancies in terms for fish. Teutonic, Celtic, Latin are at one ; Sanskrit and Zend diverge in company. But here the argument is feeble, inasmuch as rivers breed fish equally with the sea. Oriental diet, or nomad pastoral life on the wide plains of Asia, may well have proved fatal to the word.

The names of *fauna* and *flora* next invite consideration. The subject has been thrashed almost *ad nauseam* without carrying conviction to disputants on either side, yet I cannot hold with Schrader that it is doomed to sterility. It is true that with the disappearance of an animal or tree the name assigned to it **drops** spontaneously **out of** the vernacular, and that there is little likelihood of a common name surviving the removal of all occasion for its use; and the recognition of this fact will relieve us from much fruitless and prolonged discussion. But nevertheless the consideration of the vocabulary in this respect may yield general inferences of no small value, which it will be the object of this section to deduce.

To begin with quadrupeds. The domestic animals give no results of value. The dog, the cow, the sheep, the pig, the goat and the horse all bear Indo-European names, and were known therefore, and all probably domesticated, prior to the separation of tongues. Whether the species originated, or whether they were first domesticated, in Asia or in Europe, has no bearing on the present question.

Wild animals deserve closer attention. The *lion* opens a difficult controversy. The main facts are unquestioned—that no common term connects the Asiatic and the European groups; that Indian and Eranian are themselves out of accord; while the same name is preserved in every member of the western branch. Upon the actual root employed opinions differ; some regard it as a *loan-word from Semitic,* which in *laish* approaches closely to λίς. But it seems impossible, without violence, to explain all current forms from this original, so that high authorities are disposed to trace their origin to some Indo-European root, as RAV to roar, LU or LEV destroy, or LIV dun-coloured. The tangle is perplexing. The lion is certainly associated with the East (though valid evidence attests the existence of lions in Greece into historic times), and one would have expected that so picturesque and commanding a creature once named would not have lost its title; that Asiatic emigrants would have preserved its memory, and by adaptation, if not otherwise, retained its title, even if they passed out of its range of habitation; still less would the Aryans proper have lost or changed the name. The difficulties do not end here. Assuming Semitic borrowing, it is hard to explain the uniformity of European terminology; assuming Indo-European identity acquired in Asia, it is strange that the name should have been conserved by all the stocks, except those to whom the lion himself remained familiar. The Tiger, whose range extends northwards beyond Bactria, is etymologically imported from India, and so too the panther, πάρδος and πάνθηρ both coming of late borrowing. Camel is once again exotic, and *pilu* of Sanskrit, from the Persian *pil,* has no European congener. These are the great characteristic quadrupeds of the East, for size and make and mark more notable than any other in the animal kingdom. Being non-European all may have dropped into oblivion in western speech, but taken collectively they constitute a negative argument of some small weight against the Asiatic derivation of the Indo-European family. And the wild-ass, the jackal, and the ape reinforce the argument from silence.

Passing from negative to positive evidence, we will first group the quadrupeds with names of Indo-European pedigree.* They are the *Bear* (*ursus*), *Beaver*, *Boar* (wild or tame), *Fox*,† *Hare*, *Mouse*, *Otter*, *Squirrel* (*viverra*), *Wolf*. Though for the most part indecisive, the general complexion of the list is European rather than Asiatic, and two animals, the Beaver and the Otter, seem specifically European.‡ In the latter case there is perfect correspondence of form, **Lit.** *udra* being absolutely identical with **Skt.** and **Zd.** *udra*, but in meaning, Greek, Sanskrit and Zend differ. It is *possible*, though the chance is rare, that distinct stocks fashioned independently words (identical in root and suffix) for distinct animals ; it is more likely that in districts where the otter was unknown, the designation was transferred to another animal of corresponding habitat. If so, assuredly the European otter was first owner of the superfluous name, not *vice versa*. The beaver stem shows like divergence of meaning. The beaver known to Teutonic, Lithuanian, and Latin vocabulary—though the animal seems now confined to Russia and Poland—appears in Zend as *bawri*, and in

---

* To transcribe comparative lists of words, which controversy has made familiar, seems superfluous. Where English does not give the key, I have put down one representative term for guidance.

† Fox is doubtful, and in spite of **Np.** *rôbât*, **Arm.** *aloüés*, Curtius and Spiegel both reject the equation ἀλώπηξ = **Sk.** *lōpāça*; **Lit.** *lápĕ* and *rubà* are added as European cognates. Also **Sk.** *khinkira* appears by κίρα.

‡ The wolf, I understand, does not now frequent India or Persia, but the Rigveda and Zend Avesta abound in invocations against his ravages.

THE CRADLE OF THE ARYANS.   19

Sanskrit as *babhru,* denoting an animal of the large
ichneumon kind.   Now this is precisely what might be
expected, the transference of a superfluous name (for the
beaver is strange to India) to an animal bearing a rough
general resemblance to the original.   Precisely in this way
the jackal of the East supplies the modern Greek with his
name for badger (τζακάλης).   Those who reject this account
content themselves with questioning the etymological
identity.

Snakes (*anguis*), worms (κάμπη, *vermis*), ants (**Zd.**
maoiri), flies (*musca*), and other Indo-European vermin
afford no topographical clue ; they are ubiquitous.

Before leaving the mammals, it will be well to consider
the list common to the *European group,* recognised in the
south by Greek or Latin, in the north by Teutonic, Slavonic,
or Lithuanian.   The following, as a glance at the appended
table will show, comply with these conditions :—

	Greek.	Latin.	Celtic.	Slavonic.	Lettic.	Germanic.
Badger		*taxus** (late, prob. borrowed)				O.G. *dahs*
Boar		*aper*		*v-epri*		*Eber*
	[καπροs†	*caper*				O.N. *hafr*]
Hedgehog	ἐχῖνος			*jezi*	*ezys*	O.G. *igil*
Lynx	λύγξ				*luszis*	O.G. *luhs*
Marten		*martes*				O.G. *marder*
Rabbit (coney)	κόνικλος	*cuniculus*	*coinin*			*Caninchen*
Seal	σέλαχος					O.G. *selah*
Stag	ἔλαφος		Cym. *eilon*	*jel-eni*	*el-nis*	
	κεραός ‡	*cervus*	Cam. *karw*	*kravu*	*karve*	*Hirsch*

In this branch of the discussion the importance of
European consensus has been strangely underrated or

* For the suspicions of borrowing that attach to this, and not less to the
Coney, see Hehn (ed. Stallybrass), *Wanderings of Plants, &c.,* pp. 493-4,
and p. 343.
  † Unspecified, of the male, boar or buck.   Cf. *verres.*
  ‡ The ‘ *horned,*’ and the specification is not complete, as in both Slav.
and Lit. the word signifies ‘ cow.’

ignored. These animals are known to *all* the West, though possibly unknown as well as unpreserved by languages of the East. Now the upholders of an original Asiatic home are virtually at one in assuming the separation of stock dialects in the Asiatic period,* in the regions east or south of the Caspian. Thus in the case of names common *to the whole of Europe* it is inferred that the animals were known and named on the far side of the Caspian, and the names faithfully preserved in after years by the various emigrant stocks. There is nothing in the present list to refute such a hypothesis, for the seal is a denizen of the Caspian as well as the Northern Seas, but it combines with the previous group to strengthen the impression of a European rather than Asiatic cradle of experience, and it is highly significant that *every noticeable European quadruped*, tame or wild, is included either in the Indo-European or the European unity.

Birds teach little. Besides the duck (*anas*) and goose (*anser*) which were perhaps domesticated, and omitting onomato-poetic names (such as cuckoo) which are valueless as evidence, the crane, crow, owl,† pigeon (*columba*), thrush, quail, and probably vulture (*glede*) and falcon (ἰκτῖνος and perhaps φήνη) are Indo-European, a few species, that is, singled out by size or cry or plumage or flight in the days before birds were much available for food. If there were proof that the duck and goose were not domesticated, the prominence of *water*-fowl would be worthy of remark, for to this category belongs **Sk.** *marala* (*merulus*), while both in Sanskrit and Greek the κολυμβός designates the grey diver.

For the group of water animals is more fertile in sugges-tion. The discrepancy between the generic European terms for fish (*piscis* and ἰχθύς) and the Eastern *matsya* has been paraded with some satisfaction by the advocates of Bactria.

* On this see further at p. 33.

† *Ulucus* by Sk. *uluka*, and *bubo* by Pers. *trum* are the comparisons.

"People starting from that central home in Asia," writes Max Müller, "ought to have little knowledge of fishes." The inference is flimsy. Wherever the Indo-Europeans were cradled, by river, lake, or sea, fish must have been known to them, and the discrepancy must be reckoned among the thousand casualties that have befallen speech.* More valid inferences await us in this sphere, of which the name for eel yields the most vivid illustration. *Anguilla*, ἔγχελυς, **Lit.** *ungurys*, **Sl.** *agulja*, show a common term for an animal that appears not to exist in the Black Sea or Caspian or their tributary streams. Here then, at last, we are driven to a corner, and must accept the inference that the European unity was maintained at a point clear of the watersheds of the Euxine and the Caspian, that the ancestors of Greeks and Italians were in touch with ancestors of Slavs and Lithuanians at some point in Central or Western Europe which the evidence forbids us to place far east of Russia's western frontier. This, if tenable, will prove decisive to the whole controversy.

Among water animals attesting an Indo-European unity is the crab (**Sk.** *karka*, κάρχα, *krebs*, **Sl.** (*k*)*rakŭ*); while European unity appears in the lobster (κάμαρος, [*homarus*], *Hummer*), the seal (σέλαχος, **O.N.** *sel-r*), perhaps the mussel† (*musculus*), and the oyster. The latter (ὄστρεον, *ostrea*, **Cel.** *oestren*, **Sl.** *ostrei*), Max Müller imputes to borrowing, claiming Greek for the original: but of the rest it is difficult to credit that they were carried from the Caspian as a common heritage by stocks so widely divergent as the

---

* The three groups—
　　　Sk. *matsya*, Zd. *masya*, N.P. *māhi*,
　　　piscis, Got. *fisks*, Ir. *iasc*,
　　　ἰχθύς, Arm. *tzukn*, ? Lit. *zuvis*, (? Ա)
suggest derivation from specific fish, familiar or favourite in given areas; none of them represents a common verbal root, 'swim' or the like.

† Sk. *çankha*, κόγχος, *congius* is of precarious meaning.

Teutonic and the Greek. On the opposite assumption, that of European origin, their disappearance (except the crab, which has land representatives) was inevitable in the Eastern tongues. In so far they corroborate the evidence supplied by the eel.

Passing from *fauna* to *flora*, we find the beech giving rise to vehement and frequently mistaken controversy.* A common name (φηγός, *fagus*, *buocha*, *beech*, and the unproved **pers.** *būk*) appears throughout the Western group, and is in many of them applied to the beech. The Eastern limit of the tree in Europe appears to be marked by a line drawn roughly from Königsberg past the East Polish frontier to the Crimea. Thus the community of name, assuming its primary association with the beech, becomes of great importance to the secondary issue in showing that the united Aryans, *if of European origin*, came not from Rokitno marshes or Russian steppes, but from some more Westerly district: but seeing that it reappears in Asia Minor, † and skirts the South shores of the Caspian, it can contribute nothing to the main issue of European or Asiatic origin. The birch and probably the pine (πίτυς) are genuinely Indo-European, but grow equally in Asia and Europe. The evidence is quite insufficient to show that either the oak ‡ (δρῦς, **Sk.** *dru* = wood, **Zd.** *dru* = shaft, *tree*), ash (*ornus*, **Sk.** *arna*) or fir attained (or retained) identification in the Asiatic group, while the common name for withy (*vitis*), and probably too *populus*, by **Sk.** *pippala*, is descriptive rather than generic. Common to widely severed European stocks, Northern and Southern, are names for the alder (*alnus*), apple, ash, elm (*ulmus*), fir (ἐλάτη), hasel (*corulus*),

---

* See letters in *Times* of October 10, 12, 14, 15, 18 (1887).

† Schow, *Botanical Atlas*; Drude, *Atlas der Pflanzen-Verbreitung*. Pl. IV.

‡ *Dru* is clearly inconclusive, and βάλανος, *glans*, **Arm.** *kalin*, does not define a particular tree.

maple,* pine (πεύκη), willow (*salix*), yew (*taxus*), and other trees. As with the quadrupeds, so here, the list goes far towards exhausting the common and conspicuous trees, truly indigenous to Europe.† Once more is it likely, is it credible, that the unity is due to a hypothetical period of common speech to South or East of the Caspian? It has all the marks of North or Central European derivation. One of the number, πεύκη, is of special interest; for while in Greek, Lithuanian, and Old German (*fiuh-ta*, whence *Fichte*), it represents fir, it is applied in Sanskrit to the betel-nut palm. How naturally this transference of name would come about upon the theory of European origination is obvious.

As for cereals, rye and barley, **Sk.** and **Zd.** *yava* by ζειά, **Lit.** *java*, **Celt.** *corna*, and again **Zd.** *gurtak* by κριθή, *hordeum, gersta*, are the only Indo-European terms, and the latter is unspecialised to barley in the East. Those who are content with Geiger ‡ to build on the evidence of silence, argue that for the cradle of the speech we must select an area suitable for barley and rye, but not for wheat, and urge North Europe upon this ground. But the conclusion cannot stand upon its own merits, and is more than usually precarious in making no allowance for agricultural as well as climatic conditions. That it accords with this hypothesis is all that may be said. To extend the argument further to the vetch (*ervum* and *cicer*), κάμαρος, *malva*, and other Indo-European or European plants would add nothing to our main results. The term for hemp (**A.S.** *haenep*, κάνναβις) shows complete Indo-European equivalence, but structure and form of correspondence indicate borrowing rather than primitive identity, and its origin is probably exotic.

---

* *Ahorn* seems *borrowed* from *Acer*, but *klen* stem connects Slavonic, Lithuanian, German, Celtic and Greek. Hehn, *Kulturpflanzen, Anm.* § 71.

† Heyn shows how many of our common trees, chesnut, sycamore, cypress, laurel, and others, are imported from the East within historic times.

‡ *Development of Human Race*, p. 145–6.

IV. Primitiveness of Type.

Primitiveness of type is another argument upon which advocates of the Asiatic theory, and conspicuously Professor Max Müller, have strongly insisted in support of their case. But in truth the argument as usually put is fallacious, the inferences in large measure unwarrantable, and the facts are now passing over to the enemy. The argument may be stated thus :—The Eastern languages, particularly Sanskrit, are the most primitive, that is to say, exhibit the closest fidelity to the original type. Primitiveness of form implies proximity to source of derivation. Therefore the cradle of Indo-European speech is to be looked for in the East.

First for the main assertion, that Sanskrit is the most primitive in type. Of morphology it still holds true that Sanskrit exhibits a larger number of the inflectional forms, and closer adherence to the original type, than any of the cognate languages. It preserves intact for instance the seven cases of the Indo-European noun. But recent years have greatly weakened the argumentative force even of this plea. Schleicher and his school largely reconstructed the inflectional system of Indo-European out of Sanskrit materials, with the result that the primitiveness of Sanskrit was exaggerated out of all just proportion. The revision of their results, necessitated by the progress of research, has revealed that there is hardly a language, if indeed one at all, which does not at important points adhere more closely to the archetype than the Sanskrit of 3,000 years ago. There are philologists of repute who claim for Celtic, and still more for the Lithuanian group,* a primitiveness exceeding that of Sanskrit itself. What is true of morphology,

* Whitney for instance, *Language and the Study of Language*, p. 203, writes :—"Of all the existing tongues of the whole great family, the Lithuanian, on the Baltic, retains by far the most antique aspect;" and in the same sense Pösche, *Die Arier*, and in the main Cuno.

might with justice be repeated of sematology. But when we come to the all important sphere of phonology, the tables are completely turned. Schleicher crudely constructed his vowel-scale upon a Sanskrit basis, and regarded the European *e* and *o* as modifications of the original and uniform *a* conserved by Sanskrit. The doctrine is now disproved, and it is matter not of conjecture but of demonstrated fact that the European stocks have adhered more closely to the Indo-European system of vocalisation than either of the great Eastern groups. In fidelity to the triple vowel *Ablaut*, Greek stands immeasurably nearer to the archetype than Sanskrit; so too to a lesser extent does Lithuanian. Of the guttural series the like is true. * Sanskrit, even in preserving traces of original differences of utterance, has travelled further from the archetypal sounds than almost any European group. These phonological facts are far-reaching and fundamental; though to some extent obscure and difficult in their bearing upon the controversy in hand, they go deeper than morphological divergence or correspondence; for this reason—that they, if any, rest on physiological modifications. It is hard to believe that climate or physical structure acts very directly on morphology; in the sphere of phonology on the other hand it cannot but be active, and a revolutionised system of articulation is a far weightier argument for changed localisation than any tenacity of grammatical or morphological instinct can counterpoise.

A further claim to primitiveness on behalf of Sanskrit rests on the simplification or clearer definition of the *Root* elements in words. With those who can still hold to a belief in the genesis of language from monosyllabic roots, verbal and pronominal, by aid of agglutinative processes, this plea will have weight. But that chimera is doomed; accumulating evidence shows that the progress of language is

* A fuller statement of this is reserved for p. 59.

a development from confusion into system, from multiplicity towards simplicity, from caprice into conformity. So is it with sounds, with word-building, with roots. Language is the outcome of slow selective instinct, a residuum of number-less experiments and ventures. The Sanskrit alphabet is but a remnant of Indo-European sounds; suffixes and inflections are survivors of a discarded host of superfluities; and so too the logical development of a system of roots and stems, in so far as it is not the retrospective analysis of the grammarian, implies distance rather than proximity to the parent type, in which it is matter of demonstration that no fixed forms had crystallised.

But further, and not less important, qualifications of the argument are necessary. The conditions of comparison must be tested; and among the most important of these is the relative age of the languages compared, the distance in time that separates them from the archetype, and the corrup-tive forces to which they have been exposed. Between Sanskrit and old Celtic, or between Zend and Slavonic no just comparison can be instituted. They represent periods of dialectic variation separated by centuries, and realised under very different circumstances. The language of the Vedas anticipates by centuries the first recorded accents of Celtic or Teutonic, of Slavic or Italic stocks, and serves only to give some measure of the changes wrought by the corrosion and denudation of those centuries in the unwritten vernaculars of kindred tongues. It is not even possible to establish any equation between growth in intel-ligence and conservatism in linguistic habit. The savage Celt retained much of morphological elaboration that the cultured Greek lost. Concurrently with the most rapid development of national culture, English divested itself of the whole system of inflections which was its morphological heritage. The one truth that seems to emerge is that conservatism in language rests far more upon the creation of a recognised norm—of a literature, that is, whether oral or written—than upon any mere lapse of time or change of domicile, or even of physiological habit. This is the prime antiseptic, as shown in the history of Greek, of Slavonic, of Latin, of English, of the Romance Languages, one and all. Sanskrit is most faithful to primitive forms, in so far as it first and nearest to its source attained literary permanence.

But assuming the primitiveness of Sanskrit, what deduction can it warrant? Schleicher, basing his theory on purely linguistic and mainly morphological lines of argument, and assuming an Asiatic derivation, maintained that throughout the Indo-European languages the more easterly the geographical position of a language, the closer was its adherence to primitive forms and sounds, and that, conversely, the further west a language had migrated, the earlier was its detachment from the common original. Further study of Celtic revealed to him the formidable infringements of this generalisation, which the phenomena of that group present; and modern phonology has annihilated it. It does not even rest upon any sound general principle. There is nothing to show that a tribe upon the move modifies its language faster or slower than a tribe at rest. There is no fixed equation between language-change and place-change. Language-structure as yet gives us no information, whether Sanskrit or Celtic has travelled furthest, or what circumstances or ethnical characteristics induced greater fidelity to type in one case than in the other. Assuming that language depends ultimately on physiological causes, dependent in their turn upon stability of environment and type, there is a probability that the race which remains in undisturbed possession of its first home will deviate least from the archetypal sounds and forms of speech. But even here unknown disturbances, such, for instance, as the infusion of new race elements, must render the argument precarious; and how cautiously it should be used, Sanskrit itself attests with emphasis. If one thing is more certain than another, it is that the forefathers of Sanskrit-speaking folk framed their language in presence of winter colds unknown to torrid India; another is that the Indian stock entered India by migration from the north-west, and that the Eranian or Persian stocks— *whatever* the original habitat of Indo-European speech—stood nearer to the locality and the environment of the original race, than the occupants of India. In spite of which, the Zend of the Persian diverged far more widely from the archetype than the Sanskrit of the Indian. Linguistic primitiveness is ineffectual to prove proximity of local origin.

V. *Differentiation of Stocks.*

The next head of the argument concerns the dispersion of the original Indo-European into clearly marked linguistic stocks, the relation of the different stocks, the order, and (so far as they can be traced) the routes of migration.

Our starting point in this enquiry must be the proved linguistic relationship between the different families of speech. All minor details, and all modern developments that fall within the ken of history may be ignored. It will be enough to consider the great main divisions of speech— Indian, Eranian, Armenian, Greek, Italic, Celtic, Germanic, and Baltic-Slavonic. In comparing these, clearness of differentiation is the first striking feature. Familiarity robs it of strangeness, but the absence of connecting links between type and type is a curious phenomenon; separation of types must have been gradual, following the ordinary course of dialectic variation, and the extreme divergence attained clearly implies the extinction or absorption of many intermediate types, such as Macedonian or Phrygian might, if surviving, have exhibited. The relationship between the survivors presents a problem full of perplexity. Phonology, morphology, vocabulary, yield distinct and often opposed results. Different resemblances have impressed different inquirers, and the doctors differ irreconcilably concerning the true order of affinity. Max Müller, Fick, Spiegel, content themselves with the broad division into Asiatic (Aryan) and European : Lottner, Schleicher, Justi, insist upon the divergence of the North from the South European group, coupling the latter with the Eastern stocks : while Hübschmann's association of the Letto-Slavonic group with Armenian and the Aryan branch throws an apple of discord between these two broad groupings. To enumerate hypotheses is tedious. Greek may be selected as a single example. Schleicher upheld a Græco-Italo-Keltic period, and the morphological resemblances of the Italian and Celtic types unite them closely. Mommsen and Fick give the weight of their high authority to the existence of a distinct Græco-Italic stage, with progress in agriculture for one of its specific marks.* On the other hand, the alliance between Greek and Armenian is undeniable, and at many points, in religion and mythology even more conspicuously than etymology, Greek stands in far closer relationship with Sanskrit than with any of the Italian dialects. To classical students, the intimate correspondence of Greek and Sanskrit in their inflectional systems, alike of noun and verb, must appeal with commanding force :—in the verb for instance, the preservation of -μι forms of conjugation, the distinction of Thematic and non-Thematic formations, the survival of the dual, with etymological correspondence even in minute vowel-variations, the

---

* Mommsen, *Hist. Rom.*, ch. ii. Hehn and Helbig contest this theory, and regard the resemblances as European rather than specifically Græco-Italian.

entire system of middle personal terminations, the retention of the augment, &c., &c.—features wholly, or almost wholly, obliterated in Latin and other European stocks. In truth it is absolutely impossible to deny the reality of the observed affinities. Aryo-Greek, Slavo-Iranian, Germano-Slavic, Germano-Celtic, Italo-Celtic combinations, all rest on solid evidences. What is the key to the puzzle?

The old idea of *lineal* descent and relationship must be abandoned. Schleicher, under the sway of biological preconceptions, regarded the differentiation of languages as analogous to that of species, assuming a common ancestor, fission of a dialect or group of dialects at a given point, and ultimate estrangement by process of continuous divergence. Were this conception true, it could be traced and verified : the line of succession and the order of severance determined. The facts necessitate a readjustment of view. There is no relationship of direct lineal succession between the stocks ; this indeed was long ago perceived : but beyond this, there was no divergence, or rather divarication, at a given point in time or place. Rather there was progressive differentiation, realised under conditions of intermittent contact and reaction. This theory is rather fancifully described by Schmidt as a ' wave-theory ' of language.* It conceives the problem thus. Indo-European speech does not (within linguistic purview) begin as a single homogeneous dialect spoken at a single centre, and radiating lineally thence ; the original Indo-European of the philologists is rather a widely distributed body of speech, extending over a large area of country, possessed of the strong general resemblance due to common descent, such as that exhibited by the yet more widely severed members of the Turko-Tataric family. In common with all languages, it was subject to dialectical variation of every degree and kind. Distinct areas, due to

* *Verwantschaftsverhältmisse der Indo-Germanischen Sprachen*, p. 27.

geographical configurations, or tribal relationships, or other more fortuitous centripetal influences, gradually formed themselves, obeying different laws of dialectical variation, and acted on by different determinants in the form of climate, surroundings, occupation. and, in all probability, alien forms of aboriginal speech. And in this connection it is important to observe the large allophylic element incorporated into the various Aryan tongues, as though each branch had made its individual appropriations from foreign sources. In Greek, for instance, Wharton estimates that out of more than twenty-seven hundred primary words fifteen hundred only can be with any probability referred to Indo-European origin.* For long these distinct areas, destined to develop the different families of speech, were not severed by hard and fast barriers of speech. There was overlapping of area on area, play and counter-play of phonetic tendency, interchange or unconscious co-operation in the work of word-manufacture. The *rapprochement* between group and group was sporadic, variable, and discontinuous, influences coming sometimes from one side, sometimes from another. Such is the sure inference that comparative philology supplies.

Thus viewed, the relations of the various groups become fairly explicable, and it seems possible to determine approximately which areas of speech came within range of mutual influence. A disposition somewhat like the following leaves no important problem of affinity unexplained. Minor readjustments are possible *nach Belieben;* if any one, for instance, believes strongly in a specific Germano-Aryan or Italo-Aryan connection, it would be possible to introduce it, but either lacks linguistic warrant.

While in general accord with the geographical distribution

* Sayce, *Address to British Association,* 1887. It would be a laborious and delicate task to ascertain the extraneous element in each of the great stocks, but would yield important results in determining relative fidelity to the parent speech and essential purity of strain.

of stocks, the diagram satisfies all the salient affinities that language attests.   It explains the broad separation between the northern and southern European types ; it reconciles with that the proximity of Celtic to Italic.   It places Greek in right proportionate relation to the Italic, Armenian, and Aryan (especially Indian) groups, and it yet shows how the Aryan, and more particularly the Armenian and Iranian type,

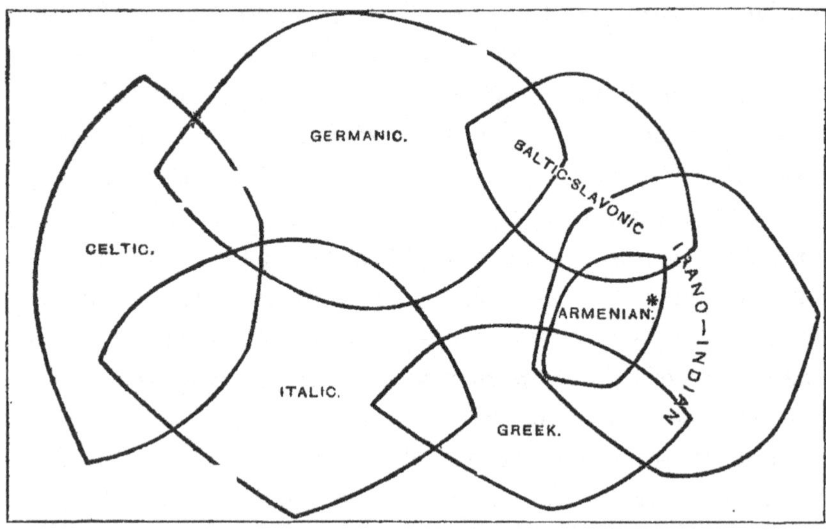

may have shared with the Letto-Slavonic a large phonetic tendency or contagion, such as that which has resulted in the parallel sibilation of the guttural series, which is common to the two groups.†

What bearing has this reconstruction upon the original habitat of Indo-European ?   It makes strongly and almost conclusively for a European habitat, situate west of the

* Armenian very probably represents a later migration, derivative from Græco-Phrygian stock., by emigration perhaps not earlier than 700 B.C.

† This and other instances of telling phonological correspondence are treated more completely, p. 59–69.   For proportionate correspondence in vocabulary between East-Aryan and the separate European stocks, tables in Schmidt's *Verwantschaftsverhältmisse der Indog. Spr.* give useful data.

Caspian and north of the Caucasus. Great physical obstructions such as these interpose natural linguistic barriers, which would check free interaction between the separated areas. Not one of those who uphold an Asiatic origin has proposed any arrangement that satisfies the linguistic conditions of the problem. Take Lenormant's as one upon which it would be difficult to improve. The cradle of the Eastern stocks he places to north-eastward, on the borders of Sogdiana, whence they passed respectively to Persia, and, *via* Kabulistan, to India. Prior to this migration the European sections had felt the westward impulse. In Bactria lay the Graeco-Italic tribes, who, clinging for a while together, passed by Herat, Khorassan, and Asia Minor to their European peninsulas. The Celtic branch, issuing from a more northern cradle, say Margiana, and moving south of the Caspian, crossed the Caucasus, skirted the Black Sea, and so passed on to the Danubian basin and Central Europe. The Germano-Slavic sections, fording the Oxus, and keeping to latitudes above the Caspian, traversed the Scythian steppes into N. Europe. The whole of this is ingenious speculation, devoid of corroborative evidence from mythology, history or archæology. And from the linguistic side it signally breaks down. For instance, it contradicts the broad European unity that exists in the general fabric of language, and more specifically in the nomenclature of trees, animals, and agriculture. It gives no account of the unique relationship between Greek and Sanskrit, and it implies a tie far closer than exists between Greek and Latin. It gives no explanation of Latin and Celtic correspondences. It puts the German stock entirely out of touch with the Celtic, and it would naturally imply German participation in all phonetic idiosyncrasies shared by Letto-Slavonic with the Aryan (*i.e.*, Asiatic) types. The breakdown could not be more complete.

There remains a single point. In whichever direction the

migration took effect, the barrier of the Caucasus and Caspian would be likely to impose a specific unity upon the tribes who crossed it in company. Of this there is very little to be traced in the European family regarded collectively. High authorities consider southern European stocks to stand in closer relation with Aryan than with north European. But the Aryan family do exhibit a close resemblance, and, moreover, just of that kind which active companionship would supply. The correspondences with their Western kin are broad and fundamental, and consist in ingrained habits, phonetic or morphological; their correspondence with one another is in the sphere of vocabulary, as though at some later stage they had lived joint lives, and experienced common vicissitudes, and together moved in new surroundings.* Assuming that their Indo-European contact lay in the West, and that at some later date they passed the Caucasus together, or in one another's train, the specific unity† of the united Aryan stock falls into its natural place.

There are incidental corroborations of these views upon the linguistic side, negative indeed and to some extent precarious, but deserving of mention as giving cumulative support and coherence to the argument. The theory of Asiatic origin generally, if not in all hands, postulates an advance through Asia Minor of at least the Græco-Italic stock. But all traces of Aryan speech recovered from Asia Minor seem clearly derived from European immigrations, such as the traditional passage of the Phrygians from Thrace, and not a trace is left of any pristine Aryan names or vernacular.‡ Of Armenia, Media, Susiana, the very countries

---

* Cf. common terms for Eastern animals, and common losses, as of "sea," "fish," etc. Any chapter of Spiegel, *Arische Periode*, supplies numerous and telling illustrations.

† This is the one factor not fairly met and elucidated by the foregoing diagram, which shews the prior stage only.

‡ Should Hittite, as is now whispered, turn out to be of Aryan lineage, this section of the argument will need readjustment.

to which the ancestors of the great European stocks are assigned, the same is true. The evidence is positive that the population and speech of these districts was Turanian. Neither Accadian nor any of the allied languages appears to exhibit a trace of Indo-European influence. The Aryan languages that do make their appearance in this quarter show Iranian, not European affinities. Thus, in its accepted form, the Asiatic hypothesis requires us to believe that many centuries B.C., at a time, indeed, not so very far distant from the clear differentiation of stocks, the language whose representatives were vigorous and numerous enough to overspread the whole of Europe, had not only abdicated possession of its native soil, but had perished absolutely without leaving a trace among the rivals to which it succumbed. So formidable is the assumption involved, that Sayce,* in the days when he still felt tied to the accepted theory of Bactrian descent, fell back upon the desperate alternative of carrying the whole European migration round by a route north of the Caspian Sea.

Semitic joins hands with Turanian in rebutting the Asiatic theory. The latest authorities are disposed to assign to the prehistoric movements of the Semitic race a direction from the North, instead of from Arabia or the South, and Kremer derives the first migrations from the very plains, west of the Pamir plateau, between the Oxus and Jaxartes streams, which are claimed as the cradle of the Aryans. If this be so, or even had Aryan and Semitic been neighbour languages in Asia, the probability is that marks of relationship or obligation would have established themselves in the two languages. Hommel maintains that such exist, and rests his proof on the following analogues :—

---

*App. I to *Principles of Comparative Philology.* In the Preface to his latest edition, the Professor unreservedly adopts the theory of European origin, advocated in his Address at the British Association, 1887.

Ind.-Eur. …staura	*k*arna	laiwa, liw	gharata	sirpara,	waina
Semitic…… *t*auru	karnu	labi'atu, libatu	*h*arûdu	ṭarpu	wainu
(ox)	(horn)	(lion)	(gold)	(silver)	(wine)

but neither the class of words adduced, nor their phonetic correspondences, are able to sustain so momentous an inference.[*] Van den Gheyn recurs with frequent emphasis to primitive Aryan and Semitic intercourse, and asserts their anthropological unity. But nowhere does he buttress his assertions with solid arguments, which would be invaluable for the settlement of the controversy.

VI. *History.*

To this prehistoric controversy, history can make but indecisive contributions : first, the hearsay evidence of national tradition, in the form of legend and mythology, unauthoritative, yet entitled to a hearing ; secondly, those broad analogies which may tend to support, or to discredit, views advanced on independent grounds.

Chinese history was once alleged, in recorded movements of the Hiongnu and the Yeta tribes, to chronicle the latest westward migrations of our Indo-European progenitors ; but the identification of these tribes with Huns and Getai (forerunners of the Gothic stock) appears to be generally abandoned,[†] and they are now regarded as Thibetan tribes, without the smallest claim to Indo-European connection. Spiegel,[‡] the first living authority upon the subject, is equally positive in rejecting the view first popularised by Lassen, that in its *Airyanem vaejo* the Vendidad records a fixed tradition of descent from the wintry uplands of Central Asia. No hint connects it with a belief in previous national migration. Geographical bearings it has none, but Ariana,

---

[*] For discussion, see Max Müller, *Biographies of Words*, &c., 111 pp.
[†] Spiegel, *Arische Periode*, p. 5.   [‡] *Arische Periode*, 122 pp.

when located, lies to north-west, not to north-east. It is a land of pure myth, parallel to that of the Hyperboreans of Greek fable, but with localisation more vague, and associations more fabulous. History, when first it finds voice, shews the Persian races *advancing* northwards, and gives no hint of prior movements in the converse direction. From that day to this, Eranian dialects appear to have been pushing slowly northwards, and now range across Turkoman territory to Khiva and Bokhara, with feelers extended north and north-eastward of the Oxus towards the great Pamir plateau. Here their modern limit is attained, and there is not the smallest indication of tradition, of history, or of linguistic inference, that their infancy was nursed amid the inhospitable uplands of Pamir. Explorers have at length, in recent years, partially penetrated these unknown wilds. So far from furnishing corroborations of the conjectures of the old school, their reports shew that few places in the globe could furnish a more unlikely cradle for the prolific race, with which it was in ignorance accredited.

There are other members of the Indo-European family, whose earliest memories are of some worth, particularly the Indian and the Greek. The hymns of the Rig Veda, like the chapters of the Avesta,* are the voice of an invading race winning its way forward among strangers of alien race and religion. India (whatever hypothesis of prior habitat is favoured) was entered by its north-western passes, and these earliest utterances prove that, at a period† ranging from 1000–600 B.C., the memory of migration was still fresh, if not still in course of accomplishment. One other literature,

---

* On the Aryans of the Avesta as a conquering and usurping race, and, as it would seem, a race of pastoral habits, as opposed to the nomad hordes of the steppe, see Geiger's *Civilisation of Eastern Iranians*, pp. 19–22, 25 pp.

† "For myself, I have grave doubts whether the invasion was earlier than the eighth or even the seventh century B.C." Sayce, British Association, 1887.

that of Greece, carries us back to a like date. Apart from all controversies as to date of final composition, the Homeric poems carry us back to an era not posterior to 1000 B.C. Though the existence of an aboriginal (Pelasgic, or other) population is implied, there survives no distinct consciousness of national immigration. The Greeks are already in possession of their eventual home ; and there is little doubt that they entered it, as Kiepert holds, from the European north, breaking through and dispossessing Illyrian predecessors, rather than creeping along the Aegean coasts from the Hellespont and Asia Minor. Curtius' theory, that Greece was colonised from Asia Minor, has gained no favour, and general credence is given to the established tradition * that Thracian immigrants occupied Asia Minor, and that the Phrygians were an offshoot of the same stock, by emigration from the confines of Macedonia. It is a conjecture, favoured by tradition and corroborated by the scanty remains of language, that the Armenians likewise represent an earlier prehistoric emigration from the European continent. However this may be, we attain at least a valuable result of relative chronology. The Greeks were in immemorial possession of their peninsula at the time when the Indian Aryans were still annexing theirs. Facts must be tortured to reconcile this with the hypothesis of Asiatic origin. The evidence from Italy, though less early and less precise, makes in the same direction. Further historical indications, or, to speak more strictly, analogies, are submitted in presenting Dr. Penka's theories (p. 54). Here it is enough to insist on the broad fact that neither the location nor the movements of the European stocks, when emerging into the twilight of history, give the slenderest support to the theory of an immigration from the East.† In the time of Herodotus, the Slavs were

* Herod. vii. 73.

† Schrader, *Sprachvergleichung &c.*, ch. ix.

in settled occupation of Gallicia or West Russia; German stems, somewhat later, are found occupying their ancestral territory from the upper Rhine to the borders of Dacia. The Celts, prior to the time of Cæsar, are in occupation of Gaul, and the notices that survive testify to expansion east-ward or south-eastward into Switzerland and the adjacent lands, not to recession westward, such as the theory of Asiatic immigration is accustomed to assume. Pressure and movement are uniformly from the North, not from the East. The backwave of Celtic expansion south-eastward probably reflects pressure upon their own north-eastern frontiers.

Here would naturally follow the evidences from mytho-logy. But comparative mythology is still an uncleared waste of multitudinous controversy. Regarding the broadest issues there is no approach yet to agreement. The con-sanguinity of Greek and Sanskrit gods, the almost complete divorce between Greek and Italian, the relation of Teutonic and Norse mythology to that of the South European or the Asiatic groups, are riddles still unsolved.* Invaders who imposed their language, may nevertheless have adopted the gods of the people whom they subjugated. Which mythology is primitive, which derivative, which borrowed and posterior, not even experts can affirm. It seems rather droll to find the time-honoured dragon taken seriously in this controversy. M. Löher claimed his support for the European theory, but Van Gheyn says, that since the quaternary period Europe has disagreed with the greater saurians, which however throve in the Caspian and Central Asia, and are chronicled by the annalists of China !

VII. *Language and Race.*

Such then are the conclusions attainable from the study of linguistic phenomena alone. Is it possible to define still

* Wolzogen tries to prove Sanskrit mythology primitive, Norse derivative.

more closely the cunabula of the original stock? The hope of doing so depends upon the possibility of co-ordinating the results of linguistic study with the conclusion reached by independent lines of research, pursued by the ethnologist or palæontologist. For any such combination Max Müller emphatically holds that the time is not yet ripe; that for the present philologist and anthropologist must work on in isolation, following and determining their separate clues, trusting that at last their separate strands may converge in one. Yet that an eventual synthesis exists between philology and ethnology is certain; that it is discoverable is at least possible; and the time seems to have come to attempt constructive co-ordination. Even a false synthesis has its advantages, for its demolition will pave the way for some better substitute. A working hypothesis serves as a useful criterion, though it can only command assent by the cumulative support of collateral proofs.

There is much to encourage the attempt. On the one hand, there is the established unity of the European brotherhood of languages. Familiarity alone has dulled the sense of wonder at that marvellous phenomenon which a century ago would have been dismissed with incredulous derision. On the other hand, anthropologists and archæologists have been steadily reducing the number of racial varieties, which finally underlie the inextricable medley of European stocks. Few prominent anthropologists of the present day accept more than four or five at the most, and from that small total would subtract one or more as sporadic or obviously imported into some isolated corner, that for the present question may be fairly left out of account. The evidence tends to bring us back at no very distant antiquity to a Europe sparsely peopled by a very few well-differentiated types. This being so, it seems a scarcely insoluble problem to identify with approximate certainty the founders of Indo-

European speech — if once a European origin can be established from the internal evidence of language—with one out of the few alternatives open for choice. It is true that no general correlation between language and race can be maintained, and upon this ground able philologists, Oppert for instance and Hovelacque, contend that community in language affords no valid inference for asserting original affinity of race. Up to a certain point their position is incontestable. The child, of whatever race, acquires the tongue of those among whom it is brought up, and hereditary predisposition to a particular language, or even a particular phonology is, if not non-existent, so faint as to count for nothing against environment and education. It is true, further, that entire nations have in historical times adopted the tongue of foreign conquerors. In Europe, the Romance languages furnish the most conspicuous wholesale example, and the coincidence that the displaced tongue was of the same Indo-European lineage as the usurping Latin, cannot be pressed to a contention that such interchange is possible only under like conditions of affinity. In India, in Jamaica, in South America, in the Pacific Isles, the yet more radical change is being freely realised on hardly, if at all, less large a scale. But this is due to the cosmopolitan conditions of modern civilisation, on which it is needless to expatiate at length, and there is no evidence that it can be realised except where the encroaching language achieves annexation by the innate ascendency that belongs to a high civilisation in presence of an inferior, to which it is practically able to dictate. Aboriginal languages yield only to virtual exter-mination before a more powerful physical type, or to com-plete incorporation in some more highly organised form of civilisation. Now in prehistoric times there is no ground for admitting incorporation parallel to those supplied by the history of the Roman Empire, or of Islam, or of the Colonial enterprise of modern Europe. Evidence and analogy, as well as *a priori* considerations, make strongly against such a view. Savages do not on a large scale subjugate neighbour savages, build up organic empires, and impose on them their customs and their speech. The advance is gradual, and mainly physical, by slow and creeping supersession, not energetic annexation. And there is every reason to agree with Whitney that, for prehistoric times, correspondence of language gives the very strongest presumption, if not valid proof, of correspondence of descent, and that the unity of Indo-European speech implies underlying unity of stock present among the early peoples who used it. Upon this showing, it will be legitimate to use Aryan or Indo-European as a race-term, if only it is possible to decide to what race (pure or composite) it properly belongs. Against such an application Max Müller hotly, and not without some reason, protests. Aryan, to the currency of which as a linguistic term his own writings have in truth contributed so power-fully, is in his eyes the property of the philologist, minted and circulated by him with a fixed value and connotation. It has nothing to do with race; it implies nothing as to colour, tribe, or habitat. Aryans—whether black or white, dolichocephalic or brachycephalic, Asiatic, European, African, or American—are those, and those only, who use Aryan, that is, Indo-European speech. To talk of an Aryan race, or an Aryan skull, or an Aryan country, in any other sense than this is a misappropriation of terms, an infringement, so to say, of the philologist's copyright, that inevitably tends to mischievous confusions. Still, the invention of new terminology is troublous and for the most part forbidding work, beset with not a few disadvantages; and it is more important to be clear as to the sense intended than to quarrel with the form of expression. In dealing with Penka's theory, to which I now turn, it will be most convenient to adopt his own terminology, and understand by Aryan that blond dolicho-cephalic North-European race with whom he endeavours to associate the origination of Indo-European speech. Penka's two principal works, the *Origines Ariacae* and *Die Herkunft der Arier* * offer the most coherent and comprehensive synthesis of racial and linguistic descent yet propounded, and English readers may welcome a compendious statement of conclusions that have not yet been summarised in English books. It may be said in advance that his philological assertions are often rash and partisan, and at times even ridiculous; † but these incidental trips do not invalidate his main argument, while on the anthropological side there is great fulness and lucidity of statement, supported by an impressive array of authorities and facts, and commanding the eager assent of distinguished workers in that field. ‡

Recent classifications of mankind reduce the distinct types or races of man to four or three. The triple division recognises—

* To these, for brevity, I refer in later notes as O.A. and H.A. respectively.

† It is hardly possible for instance to read him seriously, when he finds (H. A., p. 23) the " Aryan " title ready embodied in Chatu-arii, Ripu-arii, Boio-arii, and the other numerous appellatives derived from the -ware (= *men*) element. Equally rash etymologising occurs in connection with the same name in O. A., p. 34, where ἀργός, *ardere*, *Armenian*, *Arii*, *Iron*, *Alemanni*, *Ermanrik* and its congeners, and even *Romani* (for Aramani), *Romanes*, and *erus* are preposterously lumped together upon a common AR or AL denoting the white or bright skin and hair of the European blond. This derivation of tribe names from colour amounts to almost a craze with him—cf. *e.g.* O.A., p. 98, on Ἕλληνες; p. 122-4 on Britanni, Belgae, Celtae.

‡ I have not adhered to the order of presentation adopted by Penka, nor refrained from free addition or omission, where it seemed advisable. The prefatory anthropological classification is from other sources, and I have only attempted to give in a few pages the gist of arguments elaborated through two volumes. Not a little of the material he uses has already been handled in earlier portions of this essay. I should perhaps add, that I am not competent to check Penka's anthropology, and space does not permit the statement of counter theories, many of which Penka himself fully states and discusses.

1. The *Ethiopian* or *Negroid*, which in this large grouping includes the *Australioid* division, which Huxley groups as a distinct fourth type, and thus covers the Negroes of Africa (Hottentots and Bushmen), the Oceanic and Melanesian Negroes, and the Negrites of the Pacific and Andaman Islands.

2. The *Mongolian*, including the natives of Northern and Eastern Asia, the Malays, the comprehensive American group, and (in an exaggerated form) the Eskimo.

3. The so-called *Caucasian*, which embraces the Xanthochroic and Melanochroic types discriminated by Professor Huxley.

This so-called *Caucasian* race, which alone is of interest for the present discussion, parts broadly into two divisions, the Northern blond type (the Xanthochroic), having for its most representative samples the people of Scandinavia, Denmark, and Iceland, and the Southern or darker (Melanochroic) type, appearing most typically in N. Africa and S. Western Asia. Between these two, and occupying all but isolated corners of Europe, are representatives of the race, showing every variety of modification that intervenes between the Scandinavian of the North, and the Arab or Persian of the South.

One somewhat too facile hypothesis is disposed to rest content with this broad triple subdivision, and to hold that in between the Negroid of the South and the Mongolian of the North, was intruded wedgewise some more favoured and highly-selected stock, provisionally styled Aryan, which, by obstinacy of physical vitality, and superiority of mental endowment, has pushed its precursors northward and southward, shouldering its way irresistibly into occupation of all Europe, and a broad fringe of Africa, and destined in the ages wholly to supersede its other human competitors. The earlier habitat of this people is conjecturally placed on or else eastward of the Asiatic and European confines of modern Russia, say the steppes northward of the Caucasus in the region of Astrakhan.

The main shortcomings of this hypothesis are twofold:— first, it fails to give an adequate explanation of the marked variations between the Xanthochroic and Melanochroic, the white and dark types of Caucasian derivation; and secondly, it fails egregiously to explain the presence of the purest specimens of the white type in N. Europe, especially Scandinavia. These two points deserve accentuation.

The White and the Dark types diverge so widely, and there is so much fixity withal in the characters of the divergence, as in the eyes of leading anthropologists to justify and even necessitate sub-racial differentiation. To account for this it is assumed, with rather easy vagueness, that the stronger infusion of Negroid* elements from the South, mingling with the pure Aryan strain, produced in varying degree and form the Melanochroic resultant; while in the North, the original Aryan retained his purity, though here and there betraying parallel Mongolian influences, tending to produce something of assimilation towards Melanochroic types. These assumptions are vitiated by fatal flaws, the most convincing of which is derived from comparison of cranial characteristics. The skull-index is in the eyes of the anthropologists the most persistent of racial mint-marks. Now the Aryans are by the hypothesis dolichocephalic in skull, like the blond whites of N. Europe, and once again the Negroid race is yet more markedly dolichocephalic; no infusion of these stocks could possibly tend towards that brachycephalism which is characteristic of the dark whites. Subsidiary objections, deduced from comparison of hair-structure, lip-formation, and facial angle may be

---

* Professor Huxley is disposed to regard the Melanochroi as a fusion between Xanthochroic and Australioid elements.

passed by. It is enough to say that there is no justification for believing that the blond white of the North, with his dolichocephalic skull-index, was ever, within approximately historic and language-making* eras, identical in race with his brachycephalic brother-white of more Southern Europe.

The second great difficulty lay in the presence of the pure blond white upon the Baltic shores. Assuming him to represent most faithfully the primal stock, it is inexplicable that starting from some distant centre, he should have conserved in a far off home, in changed environment of food and climate and ways of life, a type unable to perpetuate itself and issue victoriously from the struggle for existence in its native cunabula.

Neither however is it admissible, as a refuge from this difficulty, to regard the Melanochroic or dark-skinned white as the normal Caucasian type, and to say that the Xantho-chroic white is a modification produced through the lapse of centuries by the Northern environment—for (1) there is no proof and no likelihood that environment or latitude can in a measurable time induce such racial modifications, not only in physiognomy and tint, but also in cranial characteristic. Lapps, Finns, Eskimo, the Samoyedic tribes, in a word the whole Northern Mongolian stock, are predominantly dark, and also brachycephalic. This might be set down to greater obstinacy of hereditary physique, or to special idiosyncrasy of the Mongolian stock. But not only there, but also amongst the Welsh, the Irish, and the Highland Scotch, there is the permanent element of the dark

---

* By language-making era I allude particularly to the time to which the Aryan *Ursprache* may fairly be attributed. Without pretending to precise chronological definition, philologists generally are disposed to assign this stage to a period ranging from 1500 B.C. to 3000 B.C. Whitney, *Lang. and Study of Lang.*, p. 201, writes 2000 B.C. as an approximation. 1500 B.C. is the extreme inferior limit that the facts admit; the extension of this back-ward must be determined by analogy and divination rather than evidence.

brachycephalic type, with the anatomical peculiarities un-changed, traceable from neolithic times, and which, so far from showing signs of yielding, compromising, or disappear-ing, rather gains than loses upon its fair-skinned corrival.

And (2) the theory fails wholly to account, even to attempt to account for the sporadic appearance of the fair-skinned type in almost every country or continent peopled by Aryan-speaking populations. These significant appearances become mere random " sports," frolics of nature, springing from no assignable cause. True, they appear usually in mountain uplands—but so sporadically and capriciously, that it is impossible to find in upland life a *vera causa* for their development.* Nay, precisely to the upland conditions of Bavarian and Swiss life have been ascribed the counter-process towards dark brachycephalism, which characterises the populations of those districts.

Recognising the full intricacy of the anthropological problem, and assuming it certain that somewhere amid Aryan-speaking peoples exists the racial type, which de-veloped the language now common to all—assuming, that is, that Aryan is not Negroid, or Chinese, or Dravidian, or Mongolian by derivation—Penka first asks, What are the existent types? † They are seven in all—Indian, Iranian, S. European, Slavic, two Celtic, and the Teutonic, or more specifically, Germano-Scandinavian. ‡ The Indian and Ira-nian do not come in question where *European* ancestry is under consideration, and in no case could they be regarded as the racial progenitors of the Aryan-speaking populations of Europe. The south European type may be ignored, for

* H. A., p. 138-41.

† H. A., p. 12; O. A., p. 13.

‡ This classification, be it observed, is anthropological, not linguistic, and it is instructive to observe how closely it accords with the grouping upon linguistic grounds; it attests the power of racial idiosyncrasy in determining and individualising its proper casts of speech, whether borrowed or original.

there is conclusive evidence that the aborigines of Greece and Italy, from whom this type indubitably derives, Etruscans, Iapygians, Pelasgians or otherwise, were not of Aryan speech, but succumbed before the Italic and Hellenic immigrants. Of the two Celtic stocks, one (styled sometimes Milesian) seems associated with Cro-Magnon pedigree, and thus may be discarded. The second, in skull-index, in skin colour, and in general build, shows such marked affinities with the Slavic, that the two may be grouped together. Thus the choice practically narrows itself to the full blond dolichocephalic Teutonic on the one hand, and the shorter darker brachycephalic man of Celto-Slavonic type on the other. Of these two, one, and one only, exhibits traces of itself *everywhere* among the various populations for which philology or archæology attest Aryan antecedents. It is the last-named, the blue-eyed, fair-haired men of the Germano-Scandinavian family. Everywhere, and throughout all history, it confronts us, and challenges explanation. It appears pictorially on Egyptian monuments two thousand years before Christ. In the pages of the Rig Veda the white skins of the invading and triumphant Aryans are expressly contrasted with the black-skinned vanquished Dasyu. The earliest European historians, from Strabo to Jordanes, one after another describe the type in their portraits of Cimbrians and Teutons, Gauls and Franks, Goths and Visigoths. To-day we find it not only throughout all northern and central Europe and the British Isles, but it arrests the observer's eye among the northern ranges of the Iberian peninsula, in Italian Piedmont, in the mountains of the Peloponnese, in remarkable purity among the Sphakiots of Crete, and, passing to Africa, reveals itself in the hill-country of Algiers* and Morocco, as well as upon the flanks of the

* On the racial identity of the Algerian Kabyles with the red Celt, see Sayce's emphatic testimony at British Association, 1887.

Aures and the Atlas range. It crops out freely in the Ossets and other tribes on either side the great Caucasian range; it has its offshoots among the Tartars of the Kirghiz steppes. It reappears among the (Iranian) Galtschas of Persia, in the hill folk of Afghanistan, in the Siah Posch* or Kaffirs of the Hindu-Koosh. No other stock can claim the same ubiquity, or *ubiquity of like sporadic kind.*

This then as a first presumption might be regarded as the Aryan stock. It is the one stock which gives unity upon the *physiological* side to Aryan speaking people: is there not a likelihood that from it too derived the philological unity? With a view to determining this it is important to trace its pedigree, history and fortunes, and see how far they favour such a hypothesis.

Alone among races it can claim continuity of European development. The cranial index, which is the chief court of appeal for the identification of prehistoric European races, is dolichocephalic. This carries us back to the quaternary period.† Already in the glacial epoch, when all northeastern Europe, from Mecklenburg to Russia, lay an uninhabitable wilderness of ice, palæolithic man makes his appearance in central Europe, and his cranial index, as attested by the Engis skull,—and, indeed, all skulls securely attributable to the quaternary period—is dolichocephalic. It is to the stern environment of palæolithic man throughout these immemorial ages that Penka would attribute the original differentiation of the blond type. That primitive man was not blond is certain; that he was produced by racial differentiation, not by independent creation, men of science are now agreed; that the long-headed type may be dated back to palæolithic times, and precedes the short-headed in

---

* Van d. Gheyn, p. 26. Presence of blonds among the Siah Posch is denied by Ujfalvy, but rests on unassailable evidence.

† H. A., p. 65-8, 91-2. O. A., p. 82-5.

Europe, is the verdict of the evidence as it now stands. That it arose out of the conditions of the quaternary epoch is the natural inference. It is the outcome of the long struggle with an ice-bound world, by which European man was slowly inured to the strength of frame and the hardy resourcefulness of mind which, late in time, has secured to him the leadership of the race.

At the close of the glacial epoch, man, it would seem, like the flora which helped him to eke out subsistence, and the reindeer which was his one animal friend, moved northwards.* Such at least is the general inference drawn from the difficult problem known as the Hiatus. Between palæolithic man and neolithic lies a gulf. † Man of the quaternary stage, the so-called epoch of Madeleine, is the hunter and the fisherman, without domestic animals, without agriculture, without utensils or the rudest architectural device, as yet unable to grind or polish the split stones with which he waged his precarious struggle with the mammoth, the ice-bear, and the larger felines, which still ranged the plains and woods of Europe. With man of the neolithic period, the epoch so-called of Robenhausen, all this is changed. There is an advance that means a gap of centuries. In some localities, in parts of France for instance, in much, if not all, of Germany and Switzerland, in Austria, and as some too will have it, in Britain, the gap seems absolute; ‡ in others it is imperfectly bridged, as for instance by the Cro-Magnon men. When neolithic man appears, not only his acquisitions and his habits, but he too himself is of a different type. The long-headed skull of the quaternary drift is replaced by the short-headed of neolithic times. Avoiding long discussion on this head, and leaving on one side the

---

* O. A., p. 81-2; H. A., p. 62, 79.

† H. A., 96 pp., and cf. Boyd Dawkins, *Early Man*, p. 244, etc.

‡ H. A., p. 82.

Cro-Magnon men,[*] who, whether an original or immigrant stock, seem to have advanced from the south-west to the the occupation of France, Belgium, and the British Isles, we discern two new invading types; first, the Iberian, or Ibero-Semitic, moving upwards by way of Spain ; and—of far more import for language and for anthropology—the Turanian stock, advancing from Asia and the East, bringing with them the products and arts of Eastern civilisation, and peopling eastern and central Europe with the dark-skinned short-headed type, known as the Melanochroic, which to-day still retains the numerical superiority in Europe.

In one region of Europe, and one alone, there is evidence of a continuous development—in Scandinavia. This country presents the archæologist with problems to which different solutions have been given.[†] From grey antiquity we find there an intermixture of skulls, partly of brachycephalic, partly of dolichocephalic formation. There was a mixed population—the one a small minority, corresponding to the Mongolian type of the modern Ugro-Finnish tribes, the other in all essential characteristics to that of the modern Swede. The older interpretation assumed that the brachycephalic remains belonged to the first occupants, progenitors of the modern Lapps or Finns. But sounder research concludes that the dolichocephalic population can claim equal antiquity : that looking backward, they are of the same order as the dolichocephalic skulls that belong to the palæolithic age ; looking forward, the indubitable representatives of the mediæval Frank and the modern Swede. The theory that a

---

[*] O.A., pp. 89–94. It is disputed whether the Cro-Magnon men are referable to the palæolithic or neolithic stage. Boyd Dawkins, *Early Man*, pp. 206, 229, finds his most direct and unadulterated descendant in the Eskimo, a theory which if true gives an instructive parallel to the retreat of the blond type northward.

[†] H. A., pp. 1–10, summarise the results attained by Nilsson, Hildebrand, Montelius, Worsaae, Von Düben, and others.

population of earlier Lapps was pushed northward by the advance of the fair whites has not been confirmed; on the contrary, it appears that the Lapps eventually entered Scandinavia from the north, and that between them and southern Scandinavia lay, in these prehistoric times, an impassable frozen barrier of hill, morass, and plain, which yields no evidence of having been occupied or traversed by man at this primitive stage. The second brachycephalic order of skulls * (in percentage not exceeding ten per cent.) must represent then a pristine population that died out, or a Mongolian infusion that, as serfs or associates, formed a part of the blond Aryan community. This dolicho-cephalic race then shows here, through the stone age into the bronze age and the iron, a unique instance of continuous development. † The famous kitchen middens found on the south-eastern coasts of the Scandinavian peninsula are the imperishable record of their slow advance. Steenstrup assigns for these massed accumulations of bones and shells and other refuse, periods amounting to 10,000 or 12,000 years, through which advance is barely, if at all, perceptible. Then, whether from impulse communicated from without, or as others (Steenstrup, Engelhardt, Evans, Torrell, Montelius ‡), prefer to think, by self-development resulting from improved conditions, advance begins. The ruder implements mingle with others of superior form and finish, bearing however the stamp of a self-developing transition, not of mere importation, as elsewhere in Europe, at the hands of a more gifted invading race. The mesolithic passes to the neolithic. The kitchen-midden men become the Dolmen-builders, and the period of advance begins.

This gradual and unbroken continuity of development,

* O. A., p. 69–70.

† H. A., p. 53, 60–4, 84–6.

‡ Montelius' *Civilisation of Sweden* has recently become accessible in English through Rev. F. H. Wood's translation.

nowhere else traceable or admissible, carries with it an important inference. Had there been a great subjugation, or some overwhelming inroad of a superior race capable of supplanting and exterminating every trace of the older language, it is almost certain that here, as elsewhere, it would reveal its traces to the archæologist. But if these were Aryan-speaking men, or if development of language shared the continuity of development in civilisation and the arts, then it is certain that the direction of Aryan migration was not from Russia northwards, but in the converse dircetion; for language and archæology combine to prove that a higher stage than that of the kitchen-midden period had been attained *before* the great migration and separation of the Aryan stocks.*

Next comes, untraceable in detail whatever theory be adopted, the period of the great expansion, with its development into distinct Aryan stocks and languages. Archæology traces the Dolmen-builders of the North passing southward through France and Spain to Africa, and extending the milestones of their march even to the borders of Egypt, while in language the story of their expansion survives in the distribution of the Aryan tongues. Everywhere it was carried by the blond dolichocephalic race that was cradled on the Baltic shores; everywhere, as we have seen, in Europe, Africa, or Asia, he has left representatives perpetuating his physical characteristics. The key is found to the sporadic appearance of the type in all regions that betray Aryan influence. The hypothesis of so prolific and exuberant an expansion of a single race from this centre

---

* *H. A.*, pp. 34–6. As a side issue, the argument rebuts Pösche's hasty hypothesis of origination near the Rokitno swamps, between the Dnieper and the Bug. Anthropologically, it is quite untenable to attribute the persistent blond type of the North to local depigmentation observed over so small a district. And the theory finds no independent corroboration from either language or early remains.

seems startling. Yet there is much to support it. Always, from the very dawn of history, we are faced by the same phenomena of countless hordes of northern men streaming eastward, southward, westward, first vanquishing and then by gradual absorption coalescing with the indigenous population. The multitudinous irruptions of the Cimbrians and Teutons are but historic repetitions of the great prehistoric movements which spread the Aryan tongue and features over the European world. The records of Egypt vouch for the invasion of the country by a great European coalition,* with contingents, as it would appear, from Sicily, Italy, and Greece, in the reign of Menephtah I, which falls probably into the fourteenth century B.C. The Galatai of Asia Minor are but one less evanescent sample of myriad precursors, and themselves anticipate the Crusaders of later date. Always the early chroniclers, from Strabo and Tacitus to Ammian, Procopius and Jordanes, trace German or Celt, Lombard or Vandal, Franks or Juts, back to Scandinavia as the hive from which they swarmed. It was the *vagina et officina gentium*, the sheath and factory of nations. Movements are from the North, southward and westward, not *vice versa*. The process still continues. Since the days of Gustavus Adolphus, peaceable forms of expansion have indeed superseded the periodical inundations of armed warriors. But in new channels the incessant stream of emigration still runs on, crossing the Atlantic instead of flooding populous Europe. Always too, as a long chain of evidence shows, it is the Aryan's fate to succumb even in conquering. Only in the Scandinavian north does he retain his pristine vigour. In Norway, at this present day, the blond type remains universal, corresponding to the Germans and Franks of the earlier Christian centuries. To-day the Nor-

* On this, in its European connexions, see Gladstone's *Homeric Synchronism*, p. 141.

wegians * not only retain the old physical characteristics, but exhibit the highest average stature, the most prolific pro-ductiveness, the lowest rate of child mortality, the highest average longevity of any European race. The further we recede from Baltic shores, the less stable it becomes. In Denmark, North Germany, and the British Isles, it best maintains itself. Elsewhere it succumbs before the Turanian black-haired, short-headed type of European man.† The isolated districts where it survives are habitually high table lands or exposed sea-coasts, which most nearly approximate in climatic condition to that of the Scandinavian peninsula. High altitudes do not *produce*, but can *conserve* the blond type that has found its way there. Its capacity for successful acclimatisation is small; immeasurably inferior, for instance, to that of the Jewish stock. The hundreds of thousands of Northern barbarians who poured into Spain and Italy like a deluge, from the days of the Roman Empire to the close of the Middle Ages, have left there scarcely a trace. In France, the old Frank type is fast yielding to the Melanochroic, and is practically confined to the north. The pictures of old masters shew how far more common, alike in Italy and Germany, was the blond type only four or five centuries ago than it now is. And still the process of retrogression is visibly continuing.

In the light of these impressive facts, a theory, which novelty puts at a disadvantage, grows more credible.

To the alternative hypothesis, namely, that the Aryan language was the property of the Slavo-Celtic stock, the objections are far more formidable; they seem, indeed, insuperable. This melanochroic type ‡ appears in Central

---

* *H. A.*, 115 pp., supply the statistics.

† *O. A.*, pp. 100–4, 118; *H. A.*, pp. 120–4.

‡ *O. A.*, pp. 90–1; *cf. H. A.*, 20 pp., 31.

Europe in the neolithic, not the quaternary period. It represents a wave of Asiatic immigration comparable to that of the Huns in the fifth century, or the Mongols in the thirteenth. The proof of this rests not only on the evidence of physical conformation, but on the unassailable testimony of Nephrit axes and other implements which Asia only could have furnished. These immigrants brought with them a higher civilisation than that as yet attained by the Northern whites, and in all probability introduced into Europe the various orders of domesticated animals,* of which the dog alone appears to have been known to early kitchen-midden men. But it is almost impossible to suppose that they likewise imposed upon them their language. Not only because their racial affinities, so far as that is a trustworthy clue, imply some form of Turanian speech, but for the far more solid reason that this brachycephalic invasion never effected a lodgement in the northern regions occupied by the blond Aryans. On the contrary, whenever and wherever the two types do eventually intermingle, the long skulls appear to denote the conquering, the short, broad skull the subjugated race.† Such is the evidence gleaned from the graves, where, as a rule, the remains of chiefs are of the long-headed type. As another significant fact, strongholds become most numerous where the two types are most evenly matched, in Gaul, for instance, in Britain, and in the Dnieper district, plainly attesting the defensive struggle of an indigenous race against a dreaded invader. In the seats of the blond Aryan, and throughout North Germany, cities, strongholds or walled defences were (as Tacitus, in later times, bears witness) unknown. In the Middle Ages it still remained true, far more markedly than is now the case, that throughout Germany and Switzerland and other European countries the blond type was

* Boyd Dawkins, *Early Man*, pp. 295–300.   † O. A., pp. 20–8.

proportionately far more prevalent among the aristocracy, while the serfs remained predominantly brachycephalic. That a prolific aristocracy of immigrant warriors should have gradually established their own language in vanquished territory is conceivable; that a race of serfs should have linguistically annexed regions to which they never penetrated is an impossibility.

Such then, mainly from the racial side, is the case in favour of Scandinavia and North Germany as the cradle of Aryan speech. It finds speaking corroborations from the linguistic side. The northern cast of the common Indo-European and European vocabulary in respect to *fauna* and *flora*, and the somewhat large infusion of marine names become intelligible. It is said that every single animal, bird, or tree that belongs to the common speech is a native of the Scandinavian peninsula. The bone accumulations show remains of the *Bear, Beaver, Boar, Deer, Dog, Duck, Fox, Goose, Lynx, Mouse, Otter*, and *Wolf*, to which with some force may be added the *Eagle* and the *Swan*. The cow, goat, horse, and sheep all appear in the neolithic period, to which the development of the mother speech (*Ursprache*) must be assigned, and the civilisation of which is in striking accord with the demands of Indo-European lexicography.*

And passing from vocabulary to language-structure, certain phenomena find new and suggestive elucidation. It is well known that Ugro-Finnish dialects, though of the agglutinative order, and classed with the other agglutinative forms of Mongolian speech, show remarkable approximations to the inflectional methods of Aryan in their treatment of declensional and conjugational suffixes. The problem has been a puzzle to philologists, some of whom have actually

* H. A., pp. 34–40; and compare Montelius and Boyd Dawkins, *Early Man*, ch. viii.

regarded Finnish as attaining the inflectional stage. As we pass eastwards to the allied Ural-Altaic, Samoyedic, or Turko-Tataric populations these peculiarities disappear. Alongside of this morphological approximation, there are arresting resemblances in vocabulary, which lie deeper than mere borrowing, and affect pronominal stems, numerals, and primary verb roots.* Now anthropology shows an exact coincidence to this state of things. From very early times there must have been a strong infusion of men of the blond type among the Ugro-Finnish population, that extends eastward from Scandinavia. In Finland, the blond type appears side by side with the dark brachycephalic almost as freely as is seen for instance in Scotland or in Wales. As we move eastward the blond strain dwindles, and ere Asia is reached wholly disappears. The testimony of language and of anthropology combine to prove an early and a large infusion of the Scandinavian blonds amid the neighbouring tribes, imprinting a lasting stamp upon the physiognomy alike of feature and of speech. And the contact seems fairly traceable to a period earlier than that of the Aryan dispersion.

The reversed direction of linguistic movement involves an entire reconsideration of established views upon phonology. Within the last ten or fifteen years the phonetic assumptions of Schleicher, Curtius, and inquirers of the same school, have been revolutionised on *internal* evidence of unanswerable force, by the completer researches of Osthoff, Brugmann, Verner, and other workers in the same field. The false views were in many cases due to the assumption, then practically unquestioned, that Sanskrit and Zend represented the primitive phonology more faithfully than the Western languages. Penka claims that the hypothesis of an opposite

---

* For English summary see J. Taylor's paper at British Association, 1887, and on whole argument O.A., pp. 63-8, H.A., pp. 24-6.

movement explains much that has hitherto seemed dark. In Zend, and in Sanskrit still more completely, the primitive vowel-gradations have been more irrevocably confused and obliterated than in any of the European languages; A E O have been merged into a uniform A. The consonantal groups offer more perplexing problems, and interesting coincidences of treatment. In the guttural series * sibilation of an original *k* and *g* (palatal explosives) to *s* and *z* is found alike in the Letto-Slavonic and the Indo-Iranian groups. Penka sees in this an evidence of these two groups maintaining relation, or else being exposed to like conditions subsequently to the differentiation of groups. It finds a natural explanation in the adoption of Aryan speech by a population, whose phonetic idiosyncrasies naturally produced this modification. It is parallel to the French representation of Latin *c* by the soft *c* or *ç*; and the asserted sibilation of *k* in loan-words by the Ugro-Finnic tribes is a speaking analogy, which suggests that the change is due throughout to Turanian proclivities. Similarly, in the phenomena known as labialisation of the gutturals, as may be seen in Brugmann's † careful classification, the Eastern languages again form with Armenian, Albanian, Lithuanian and Slavonic, a distinct group contrasted with the European orders, Greek, Latin, and Teutonic. The assumption of eastward progress renders natural and intelligible a community of treatment which otherwise baffles explanation.

In the complicated question of the Aspirates,‡ Penka upholds a similar explanation. Philologists know that Greek, Sanskrit, and Iranian constantly exhibit the aspirated tenuis, where the tenuis simple appears in Celtic, Latin,

---

* O. A., pp. 139–43; H. A., pp. 50–1. For the exact representation, as contrasted with treatment in the Western groups, see Brugmann, *Comparative Grammar,* § 380.

† *Comparative Grammar,* § 417.

‡ O.A., 158 pp.

Lithuanian, and Slavic. Curtius and others maintained that the aspirate was a later development imported into the Eastern group. Penka casts in his lot with those who hold that the original language knew only aspirated mutes, and observes that to this day all North-German dialects retain in articulation the aspirated tenuis, which in the current spelling appears as tenuis simple.* He attributes the disappearance of the aspirate in the Western group to the phonetic habit of the populations Aryanised over the European area. The controversy is far too complicated for examination in these pages, and Brugmann decisively vindicates the unaspirated tenuis for the original speech, but upon any showing there remains the salient fact that Greek here groups itself with the Eastern division, a phenomenon which it is extremely hard to reconcile with any theory of Asiatic origin, which inevitably associates Greek with Italic, and exposes it to similar environment long after its separation from Indian and Iranian.

Finally, the series of sound-shiftings comprehended under "Grimm's law," the explanation of which involves such grave difficulties, is thus re-read by light of the new theory. In the Ugro-Finnic tongues neither the aspirated tenues (*ph, kh, th*) nor the aspirated mediæ (*bh, gh, dh*) find a place, while the simple mediæ, though existent, appear to have been difficult and alien sounds, in origin derivative from their corresponding tenues. This being so, it is intelligible enough that in adopting Aryan speech Turanian populations (like modern Hungarians in borrowing German terms) should have represented Aryan mediæ by the corresponding tenues, while the unfamiliar aspirates, *gh, bh, dh*, naturally enough fell to *g, b, d*.† The predominance of the Turanian strain

---

* Saying for instance, *Khind, Khunst.* Ujfalvy's contradiction of this, *Berçeau des Aryas*, p. 30, arises from phonological ignorance.

† Penka's more elaborate account of the *kh, ph, th* modification I omit, as it rests in great part on insecure hypotheses.

supplies the true explanation of the phonetic habitudes of the South-German dialects. The second great sound-shifting, affecting the High German dialects, commenced during the earlier Christian centuries, and passed from the south north-wards, representing the ground gradually gained by the Turanian element on the pure German (or Aryan) stock. It was achieved through monastic and other civilising influences, by which the darker white has gradually inoculated and superseded the blond, and in point of sound-change the supersession never became complete, taking most effect among the Bavarians and the Southern tribes most strongly permeated with a Turanian element, and least where the primitive blond stock experienced least of allophylic infusion.

Lastly, Penka appeals to mythology and legend in support of his hypothesis. In Greek literature he finds clear traces of the pristine northern home, not merely in the Odyssey at large, the structure of which Müllenhoff identifies with the German tale of Orendel, the historic hero of the Northern Sea, but more specifically still in the conception and legend of Oceanus, and in the notice of Cimmerian folk—etymologically "the men of darkness," and in history appearing as the Cimbri—"beside the bounds of swift-flowing ocean, shrouded in mist and cloud, and never does the shining sun look down upon them with his rays, neither when he climbs the vault of starry heaven, nor when he turns again from heaven's height towards earth, but deathly night is spread o'er miserable mortals*"; while the tall long-locked progenitors of the race are reproduced in the doughty Laistrygones, "a host past number, like to the giants, not men," † of whom is written the strange record :—" There shepherd cries to shepherd as he drives home the flock, and he that drives afield answers the call : there, sleep foregone, might a man earn double wage, one for herding the cows, the

* Od. xi. 14–19.　　† Od. x. 119.

other for pasturing white-fleeced flocks, so near are the out-goings of the night and of the day." *   Other unconscious obligations of Homer to Northern lore, to the phenomena of icebergs in his description of the isle of Aeolus, and to the northern legend of the ferrymen of the dead in his account of the Phæacians, would similarly be explained as confused reminiscences rather than as garbled reports gained from Phœnician mariners.

A similar origin may underlie the Persian description of the Aryas' land in the first chapter of the Vendidâd, where ' the winter months are ten, and the months of summer two, and these cold for the waters, cold for the earth, cold for the trees ; and winter falls there, with the worst of its plagues.'

In the essay in which Van den Gheyn undertakes to tra-verse the arguments of Penka, apart from partial demurrers upon the anthropological side, which Penka himself con-siders and overrules, there is little to invalidate the cumu-lative strength of the case which he has made out, and which at present offers the most complete and satisfactory synthesis that exists of problems which are scarcely likely to attain complete historic certitude.

Conclusion.

Our results may be thus summarised. The theory of the Asiatic origin of Aryan speech is devoid of solid evidence, and at present rests mainly on tradition and unfounded prepossessions. Its one solid support, the claim to higher primitiveness advanced on behalf of Sanskrit and Iranian, has broken down ; partly that the progress of philology, especially in the province of phonetics, has inva-lidated the claim itself, partly that primitiveness of type is irrelevant to local origination. The theory is beset with objections and difficulties: the absolute estrangement of Aryan from Semitic, Accadian, or other forms of indigenous

* Od. x. 81–6.

Asiatic speech, constitutes a most formidable argument from silence; the suggestions of history and the facts of geographical exploration are both adverse; the evidences of Indo-European vocabulary almost fatal; the theory precludes any rational account of the general unity of Western speech, and leaves the observed relationships between the various stocks unexplained and inexplicable. The theory of European origin elucidates all these difficulties, without creating a single new one. It tallies with the evidences of vocabulary; it explains the European unity; it allows for the gradual differentiation of stocks, and gives scope for that continued interrelation which the linguistic facts attest; it admits the observed affinities; it has the support of phonology; it is vindicated by large analogies in history; it deserves, therefore, confident acceptance. If European origin be conceded, the evidence derived from Indo-European climate, trees and fish, especially the *beech* and the *eel*, points decisively to the large northern plateau extending from the German Ocean to the confines of the Black Sea and Caspian watersheds, and this alone provides space for the wide expansion implied by the broad differentiation of dialects into separate stocks; vocabulary further implies familiarity with marine animals and the sea, doubtless the North Sea or the Baltic. So much seems well assured by successive steps of argument. Beyond this, from the nature of the materials, reasoning becomes precarious. At first sight it must appear idle guesswork to attempt the racial identification of the founders of Aryan speech. But examination shows that the possible alternatives are few, and the collateral evidences of anthropology at once more striking and more harmonious than might have been expected; and Penka has gone far towards establishing an association between Aryan speech and the race of blond whites, whose central and immemorial home is found in Scandinavia.

Made in the USA
Monee, IL
07 July 2026